Microsoft Access 2016 Keyboard Shortcuts

For Windows

By

U. C-Abel Books.

All Rights Reserved

First Edition: 2016

ISBN-13: 978-1533598943
ISBN-10: 1533598940

Published by U. C-Abel Books.

Table of Contents

Acknowledgement.

U. C-Abel Books will not take all the credits for Microsoft Access 2016 keyboard shortcuts listed in this book, but shares it with Microsoft Corporation because some of the shortcut keys came from them and are "used with permission from Microsoft".

Dedication

This book is dedicated to computer users and lovers of keyboard shortcuts all over the world.

Introduction.

We enjoy using shortcut keys because they set us on a high plane that astonishes people around us when we work with them. As wonderful shortcuts users, the worst eyesore we witness in computing is to see somebody sluggishly struggling to execute a task through mouse usage when in actual sense shortcuts will help to save that person the time wasted. Most people have asked us to help them with a list of shortcut keys that can make them work as smartly as we do and that drove us into research to broaden our knowledge and truly help them as they demanded, that is the reason for the existence of this book. It is a great tool for lovers of shortcuts, and those who want to join the group.

Most times, the things we love don't come by easily. It is our love for keyboard shortcuts that made us to bear long sleepless nights like owls, just to make sure we get the best out of it, and it is the best we got that we are sharing with you in this book. You cannot be the same at computing after reading this book. The time you entrusted to our care is an expensive possession and we promise not to mess it up.

Thank you.

What to Know Before You Begin.

General Notes.

1. It is important to note that when using shortcuts to perform any command, you should make sure the target area is active, if not, you may get a wrong result. Example, if you want to highlight all texts, you must make sure the text field is active and if an object, make sure the object area is active. The active area is always known by the location where the cursor of your computer blinks.

2. Most of the keyboard shortcuts you will see in this book refer to the U.S. keyboard layout. Keys for other layouts might not correspond exactly to the keys on a U.S. keyboard.

3. The plus (+) signs that come in the middle of keyboard shortcuts simply mean the keys are meant to be combined or held down together not to be added as one of the shortcut keys. In a case where plus sign is needed; it will be duplicated (++).

4. For keyboard shortcuts in which you press one key immediately followed by another key, the keys are separated by a comma (,).

5. It is also important to note that the shortcut keys listed in this book are for Microsoft Access 2016.

Short Forms Used in This Book and Their Full Meaning.

The following are short forms of keyboard shortcuts used in this Microsoft Access 2016 Keyboard Shortcuts book and their full meaning.

1.	Alt	-	Alternate Key
2.	Caps Lock	-	Caps Lock Key
3.	Ctrl	-	Control Key
4.	Esc	-	Escape Key
5.	F	-	Function Key
6.	Num Lock	-	Number Lock Key
7.	Shft	-	Shift Key
8.	Tab	-	Tabulate Key
9.	Win	-	Windows logo key
10.	Prt sc	-	Print Screen

CHAPTER 1.

Gathering The Basic Knowledge Of Keyboard Shortcuts.

Without the existence of the keyboard, there wouldn't have been anything like keyboard shortcuts, so in this chapter we will learn a little about keyboard before moving to keyboard shortcuts.

1. Definition of Computer Keyboard.

This is an input device that is used to send data to the computer memory.

Sketch of a Keyboard

1.1 Types of Keyboard.

   i. Standard (Basic) Keyboard.
   ii. Enhanced (Extended) Keyboard.

i. **Standard Keyboard:** This is a keyboard designed during the 1800s for mechanical typewriters with just 10 function keys (F keys) placed at the left side of it.

ii. **Enhanced Keyboard:** This is the current 101 to 102-key keyboard that is included in almost all the personal computers (PCs) of nowadays, which has 12 function keys at the top side of it.

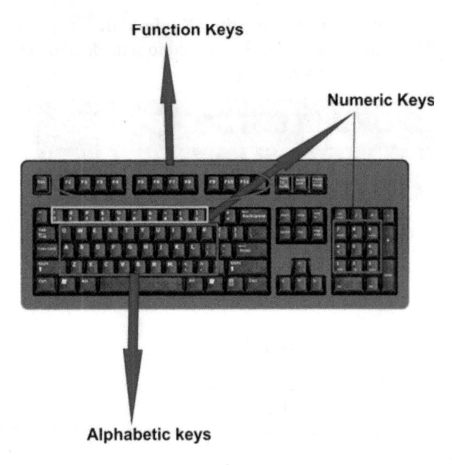

Function Keys

Numeric Keys

Alphabetic keys

1.2 Segments of the keyboard

- Numeric keys
- Alphabetic keys
- Punctuation keys
- Windows Logo key.
- Function keys
- Special keys

Numeric Keys: Numeric keys are keys with numbers from **0 - 9**.

Alphabetic Keys: These are keys that have alphabets on them, ranging from **A-Z**.

Punctuation Keys: These are keys of the keyboard used for punctuation. Examples include comma, full stop, colon, question marks, hyphen etc.

Windows Logo Key: A key on Microsoft Computer keyboard with its logo displayed on it. Search for this ⊞ on your keyboard.

Function Keys: These are keys that have **F** on them which are usually combined with other keys. They are F1 - F12, and are also in the class called Special Keys.

Special Keys: These are keys that perform special functions. They include: Tab, Ctrl, Caps lock, Insert,

Prt sc, alt gr, Shift, Home, Num lock, Esc and many others. Special keys work according to the type of computer involved. In some keyboard layout, especially laptops, the keys that turn the speaker on/off, the one that increases/decreases volume, the key that turns the computer Wifi on/off are also special keys.

Other Special Keys Worthy of Note.

Enter Key: This is located at the right-hand corner of the keyboard. It is used to send messages to the computer to execute commands, in most cases it is used to mean "Ok" or "Go".

Escape Key (ESC): This is the first key on the upper left of the keyboard. It is used to cancel routines, close menus and select options such as **Save** according to circumstance.

Control Key (CTRL): It is located on the bottom row of the left and right hand side of the keyboard. They also work with the function keys to execute commands using Keyboard shortcuts (key combinations).

Alternate Key (ALT): It is located on the bottom row, very close to the CTRL key on both side of the keyboard. It enables many editing functions to be accomplished by using some keystroke combinations on the keyboard.

Shift Key: This adds to the functions of the function keys. In addition, it enables the use of alternative function of a particular button (key), especially, those with more than one function on a key. E.g. use of capital letters, symbols and numbers.

1.3. Selecting/Highlighting With the Keyboard.

This is a highlighting method or style where data is selected using the keyboard instead of a computer mouse.

To do this:

- Move your cursor to the text you want to highlight, make sure that area is active,
- Hold down the shift key with one finger
- Then use another finger to move the arrow key that points to the direction you want to highlight.

1.4 The Operating Modes Of The Keyboard.

Just like the mouse the keyboard has two operating modes. The two modes are Text Entering and Command Mode.

a. **Text Entering Mode:** this mode gives the operator/user the opportunity to type text.

b. **Command Mode:** this is used to command the operating system/software/application to execute commands in certain ways.

2. Ways To Improve In Your Typing Skill.

1. Put Your Eyes Off The Keyboard.

This is the aspect of keyboard usage that many don't find funny because they always ask. "How can I put my eyes off the keyboard when I am running away from the occurrence of errors on my file?" My aim is to be fast, is this not going to slow me down?

Of course, there will be errors and at the same time your speed will slow down but the motive behind the introduction of this method is to make you faster than you are. Looking at your keyboard while you type can make you get a sore neck, it is better you learn to touch type because the more you type with your eyes fixed on the screen instead of the keyboard, the faster you become.
An alternative to keeping your eyes off your keyboard is to use the *"Das Keyboard Ultimate"*.

2. Errors Challenge You
It is better to fail than not to try at all. Not trying at all is an attribute of the weak and lazybones. When you

make mistakes, try again because errors are opportunities for improvement.

3. Good Posture (Position Yourself Well).
Do not adopt an awkward position while typing. You should get everything on your desk organized or arranged before sitting to type. Your posture while typing contributes to your speed and productivity.

4. Practice
Here is the conclusion of everything said above. You have to practice your shortcuts constantly. The practice alone is a way of improvement. "Practice brings improvement". Practice always.

2.1 Software That Will Help You Improve In Your Typing Skill.

There are several Software programs for typing that both kids and adults can use for their typing skill. Here is a list of software that can help you improve in your typing: Mavis Beacon, Typing Instructor, Mucky Typing Adventure, Rapid Tying Tutor, Letter Chase Tying Tutor, Alice Touch Typing Tutor and many more. Personally, I recommend Mavis Beacon.

To learn typing with MAVIS BEACON, install Mavis Beacon software to your computer, start with keyboard lesson, then move to games. Games like **_Penguin Crossing, Creature Lab_** or **_Space Junk_** will help you become a professional in typing. Typing and keyboard shortcuts work hand-in-hand.

Sketch of a computer mouse

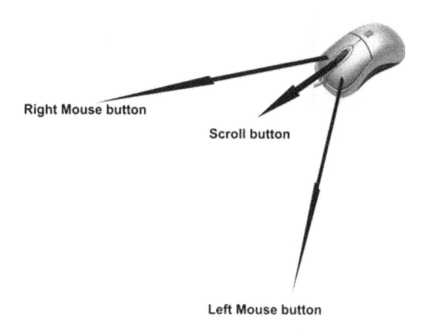

Right Mouse button

Scroll button

Left Mouse button

3. Mouse:

This is an oval-shaped portable input device with three buttons for scrolling, left clicking, and right clicking that enables work to be done effectively on a computer. The plural form of mouse is mice.

3.1 Types of Computer Mouse

- Mechanical Mouse
- Optical Mechanical Mouse (Optomechanical)
- Laser Mouse
- Optical Mouse

- BlueTrack Mouse

3.2 Forms of Clicking:

Left Clicking: This is the process of clicking the left side button of the mouse. It can be called *clicking* without the addition of *left*.

Right Clicking: It is the process of clicking the right side button of the mouse.

Double Clicking: It is the process of clicking the left side button two times (twice) and immediately.

Double clicking is used to select a word while thrice clicking is used to select a sentence or paragraph.

Scroll Button: It is the little key attached to the mouse that looks like a tiny wheel. It takes you up and down a page when moved.

3.3 Mouse Pad: This is a small soft mat that is placed under the mouse to make it have a free movement.

3.4 Laptop Mouse Touchpad

This unlike the mouse we explained above is not external, rather it is inbuilt (comes with a laptop computer). With the presence of a laptop mouse touchpad, an external mouse is not needed to use a laptop, except in a case where it is malfunctioning or the operator prefers to use external one for some reasons.

The laptop mouse touchpad is usually positioned at the end of the keyboard section of a laptop computer. It is rectangular in shape with two buttons positioned below it. The two buttons/keys are used for left and right clicking just like the external mouse. Some laptops come with four mouse keys. Two placed above the mouse for left and right clicking and two other keys placed below it for the same function.

4. Definition Of Keyboard Shortcuts.

Keyboard shortcuts are defined as a series of keys, sometimes with combination that execute tasks that typically involve the use of mouse or other input devices.

5. Why You Should Use Shortcuts.

1. One may not be able to use a computer mouse easily because of disability or pain.

2. One may not be able to see the mouse pointer as a result of vision impairment, in such case what will the person do? The answer is SHORTCUT.

3. Research has made it known that Extensive mouse usage is related to Repetitive Syndrome Injury (RSI) greatly than the use of keyboard.

4.   Keyboard shortcuts speed up computer users, making learning them a worthwhile effort.

5.   When performing a job that requires precision, it is wise that you use the keyboard instead of mouse, for instance, if you are dealing with Text Editing, it is better you handle it using keyboard shortcuts than spending more time with mouse alone.

6.   Studies calculate that using keyboard shortcuts allows working 10 times faster than working with the mouse. The time you spend looking for the mouse and then getting the cursor to the position you want is lost! Reducing your work duration by 10 times brings you greater results.

5.1 Ways To Become A Lover Of Shortcuts.

1.   Always have the urge to learn new shortcut keys associated with the programs you use.
2.   Be happy whenever you learn a new shortcut.
3.   Try as much as you can to apply the new shortcuts you learnt.
4.   Always bear it in mind that learning new shortcuts is worth it.
5.   Always remember that the use of keyboard shortcuts keeps people healthy while performing computing activities.

5.2 How To Learn New Shortcut Keys

1. Do a research for them: quick reference (a cheat sheet comprehensively compiled) can go a long way to help you improve.
2. Buy applications that show you keyboard shortcuts every time you execute an action with the mouse.
3. Disconnect your mouse if you must learn this fast.
4. Read user manuals and help topics (Whether offline or online).

5.3 Your Reward For Knowing Shortcut Keys.

1. You will get faster unimaginably.
2. Your level of efficiency will increase.
3. You will find it easy to use.
4. Opportunities are high that you will become an expert in what you do.
5. You won't have to go for **Office button**, click **New,** click **Blank and Recent** and click **Create** just to insert a fresh/blank page. **Ctrl +N** takes care of that in a second.

A Funny Note: Keyboard Shortcuts and Mousing are in a marital union with Keyboard Shortcuts being the head and it will be unfair for anybody to put asunder between them.

5.4 Why We Emphasize On The Use of Shortcuts.

You may never ditch your mouse completely unless you are ready to make your brain a box of keyboard shortcuts which will really be frustrating. Just imagine yourself learning all the shortcuts for the programs you use and its various versions. You shouldn't learn keyboard shortcuts that way.

Why we are emphasizing on the use of shortcuts is because mouse usage is becoming unusually common and unhealthy, too. So we just want to make sure both are combined so you can get fast, productive and healthy in your computing activities. All you need to know is just the most important ones associated with the programs you use.

CHAPTER 2.

15 (Fifteen) Special Keyboard Shortcuts.

The fifteen special keyboard shortcuts are fifteen (15) shortcut keys every computer user should know.

The following table contains the list of keyboard shortcuts every computer user should know.

1. **Ctrl + A:** Control plus A, highlights or selects everything you have in the environment where you are working.

    *If you are like **"Wow, the content of this document is large and there is no time to select all of it, besides, it's going to mount pressure on my computer?"** Using the mouse for this is an outdated method of handling a task like selecting all, Ctrl+A will take care of that within seconds.*

2. **Ctrl + C:** Control plus C copies any highlighted or selected element within the work environment.

    Saves the time and stress which would have been used to right click and click again just to copy. Use ctrl+c.

3. **Ctrl + N:** Control plus N opens a new window.
   Instead of clicking **File, New, blank/template** *and another* **click**, *just press* ***Ctrl + N*** *and a fresh window will appear instantly.*

4. **Ctrl + O:** Control plus O opens a new program.
   Use ctrl +O when you want to locate or open a file or program.

5. **Ctrl + P:** Control plus P prints the active document.
   Always use this to locate the printer dialog box and print.

6. **Ctrl + S:** Control plus S saves a new document or file and changes made by the user.
   Going for the mouse? Please stop! Don't use the mouse. Just press Ctrl+S and everything will be saved.

7. **Ctrl +V:** Control plus V pastes copied elements into the active area of the program in use.
   Using ctrl+V in a case like this Saves the time and stress of right clicking and clicking again just to paste.

8. **Ctrl + W:** Control plus W is used to close the page you are working on when you want to leave the work environment.

> **"There is a way Peace does this without using the mouse. Oh my God, why didn't I learn it then?"** Don't worry, I have the answer, Peace presses Ctrl+W to close active windows.

9. **Ctrl + X:** Control plus X cuts elements (making the elements to disappear from their original place). The difference between cutting and deleting elements is that in Cutting, what was cut doesn't get lost permanently but prepares itself so that it can be pasted in another location selected by the user.

> Use ctrl+x when you think **"this shouldn't be here and I can't stand the stress of retyping or redesigning it in the rightful place it belongs".**

10. **Ctrl + Y:** Control plus Y redoes an undone action.

> Ctrl+Z brought back what you didn't need? Press Ctrl+ Y to remove it again.

11. **Ctrl + Z:** Control plus Z undoes actions.
> Can't find what you typed now or a picture you inserted, it suddenly disappeared or you mistakenly removed it? Press Ctrl+Z to bring it back.

12. **Alt + F4:** Alternative plus F4 closes active windows or items.

> *You don't need to move the mouse in order to close an active window, just press **Alt + F4** if you are done or don't want somebody who is coming to see what you are doing.*

13. **Ctrl + F6:** Control plus F6 Navigates between open windows, making it possible for a user to see what is happening in windows that are active.

> *Are you working in Microsoft Word and want to find out if the other active window where your browser is loading a page is still progressing?* Use Ctrl + F6.

14. **F1:** This displays the help window.

> *Is your computer malfunctioning? Use **F1** to find help when you don't know what next to do.*

15. **F12:** This enables user to make changes to an already saved document.

> *F12 is the shortcut to use when you want to change the format in which you saved your existing document, password it, change its name, change the file location or*

destination, or make other changes to it. It will save your time.

CHAPTER 3.

Keyboard Shortcuts In Access 2016.

Definition of Program: Microsoft Access is a well-known electronic database program designed by Microsoft Corporation in 1997 which allows its users to create and manipulate database.

The following list contains keyboard shortcuts that will boost your productivity in Microsoft Access.

Access Web App Shortcut Keys

Design-time shortcut keys

These shortcut keys are available when you are customizing a web app in Access. Some of the shortcuts listed under Desktop database shortcut keys are also available when customizing a web app.

TASK	SHORTCUT
Advance through all tables and views (when not in Edit mode)	TAB
Move a table or view selector	Arrow keys
Show or hide the Navigation Pane	F11
Advance through the controls on a view (when in Edit mode)	TAB
Move the selected control(s)	Arrow keys

Open or close the properties for the selected control	F4
Show or hide the Field List	Alt+F8

Runtime (browser) shortcut keys

These shortcut keys are available when you are using an Access web app in the browser. You can also use any shortcut keys that are provided by the browser itself.

TASK	SHORTCUT
New item	N
Delete item	Delete
Edit item	E
Save item	Ctrl+S
Cancel	Escape
Edit filter	/
Close a popup view	Escape

When working in the browser, press Tab, Shift+Tab, and the arrow keys to move between the table list, the view selector, the action bar, the search box, and controls on views.

Desktop Database Shortcut Keys For Access

Global Access shortcut keys

Opening databases

TASK	SHORTCUT
Open a new database	CTRL+N

Open an existing database	CTRL+O

Printing and saving

TASK	SHORTCUT
Print the current or selected object	CTRL+P
Open the **Print** dialog box from **Print Preview**	P or CTRL+P
Open the **Page Setup** dialog box from **Print Preview**	S
Cancel Print Preview or Layout Preview	C or ESC
Save a database object	CTRL+S or SHIFT+F12
Open the **Save As** dialog box	F12

Using a combo box or list box

TASK	SHORTCUT
Open a combo box	F4 or ALT+DOWN ARROW
Refresh the contents of a Lookup field list box or combo box	F9
Move down one line	DOWN ARROW
Move down one page	PAGE DOWN
Move up one line	UP ARROW
Move up one page	PAGE UP
Exit the combo box or list box	TAB

Finding and replacing text or data

TASK	SHORTCUT
Open the **Find** tab in the **Find and Replace** dialog box (Datasheet view and Form view only)	CTRL+F
Open the **Replace** tab in the **Find and Replace** dialog box (Datasheet view and Form view only)	CTRL+H
Find the next occurrence of the text specified in the **Find and Replace** dialog box when the dialog box is closed (Datasheet view and Form view only)	SHIFT+F4

Working in Design, Layout, or Datasheet view

TASK	SHORTCUT
Switch between Edit mode (with insertion point displayed) and Navigation mode in a datasheet. When working in a form or report, press ESC to leave Navigation mode.	F2
Switch to the property sheet (Design view and Layout view in forms and reports)	F4
Switch to Form view from form Design view	F5
Switch between the upper and lower portions of a window (Design view of queries, and the Advanced Filter/Sort window)	F6
Cycle through the field grid, field properties, the Navigation Pane, access keys in the Keyboard Access	F6

System, Zoom controls, and the security bar (Design view of tables)	
Open the **Choose Builder** dialog box from a selected control on a form or report (Design view only)	F7
Open the Visual Basic Editor from a selected property in the property sheet for a form or report	F7
Switch from the Visual Basic Editor back to form or report Design view	ALT+F11

Editing controls in form and report Design view

TASK	SHORTCUT
Copy the selected control to the Clipboard	CTRL+C
Cut the selected control and copy it to the Clipboard	CTRL+X
Paste the contents of the Clipboard in the upper-left corner of the selected section	CTRL+V
Move the selected control to the right (except controls that are part of a layout)	RIGHT ARROW or CTRL+RIGHT ARROW
Move the selected control to the left (except controls that are part of a layout)	LEFT ARROW or CTRL+LEFT ARROW
Move the selected control up (except controls that are part of a layout)	UP ARROW or CTRL+UP ARROW

Move the selected control down (except controls that are part of a layout)	DOWN ARROW or CTRL+DOWN ARROW
Increase the height of the selected control **Note:** If used with controls that are in a layout, the entire row of the layout is resized.	SHIFT+DOWN ARROW
Increase the width of the selected control **Note:** If used with controls that are in a layout, the entire column of the layout is resized.	SHIFT+RIGHT ARROW
Reduce the height of the selected control **Note:** If used with controls that are in a layout, the entire row of the layout is resized.	SHIFT+UP ARROW
Reduce the width of the selected control **Note:** If used with controls that are in a layout, the entire column of the layout is resized.	SHIFT+LEFT ARROW

Window operations

By default, Access databases display as tabbed documents. To use windowed documents, Click the **File** tab., and then click **Options**. In the **Access Options** dialog box, click **Current Database** and, under **Document Window Options**, click **Overlapping Windows**.

Note: You will have to close and reopen the current database for the option to take effect.

TASK	SHORTCUT
Toggle the Navigation Pane	F11
Cycle between open windows	CTRL+F6
Restore the selected minimized window when all windows are minimized	ENTER
Turn on Resize mode for the active window when it is not maximized; press the arrow keys to resize the window, then press Enter to apply the new size.	CTRL+F8
Display the control menu	ALT+SPACEBAR
Display the shortcut menu	Shortcut menu key (near the lower right of most keyboards)
Close the active window	CTRL+W or CTRL+F4
Switch between the Visual Basic Editor and the previous active window	ALT+F11

Working with Wizards

TASK	SHORTCUT
Toggle the focus forward between controls in the wizard	TAB
Move to the next page of the wizard	ALT+N
Move to the previous page of the wizard	ALT+B
Complete the wizard	ALT+F

Miscellaneous

TASK	SHORTCUT
Display the complete hyperlink address for a selected hyperlink	F2
Check spelling	F7
Open the Zoom box to conveniently enter expressions and other text in small input areas	SHIFT+F2
Display a property sheet in Design view	ALT+ENTER
Exit Access	ALT+F4
Invoke a Builder	CTRL+F2
Toggle forward between views when in a table, query, form, or report. If there are additional views available, successive keystrokes will move to the next available view.	CTRL+RIGHT ARROW or CRTL+COMMA (,)
Toggle back between views when in a table, query, form, or report. If there are additional views	CTRL+LEFT ARROW or CRTL+PERIOD (.)

available, successive keystrokes will move to the previous view. **Note:** CTRL+PERIOD (.) does not work under all conditions with all objects.	

The Navigation Pane shortcut keys

TASK	SHORTCUT
Show or hide the Navigation Pane	F11
Go to the Navigation Pane Search box (if focus is already on the Navigation Pane)	CTRL+F

Editing and navigating the Object list

TASK	SHORTCUT
Rename a selected object	F2
Move down one line	DOWN ARROW
Move down one window	PAGE DOWN
Move to the last object	END
Move up one line	UP ARROW
Move up one window	PAGE UP

Navigating and opening objects

TASK	SHORTCUT
Open the selected table or query in Datasheet view	ENTER
Open the selected form or report	ENTER
Run the selected macro	ENTER

Open the selected table, query, form, report, macro, or module in Design view	CTRL+ENTER
Display the Immediate window in the Visual Basic Editor	CTRL+G

Work with menus

TASK	SHORTCUT
Show the shortcut menu	Shortcut key (near the lower right of most keyboards)
Show the access keys	ALT or F10
Show the program icon menu (on the program title bar)	ALT+SPACEBAR
With the menu or submenu visible, select the next or previous command	DOWN ARROW or UP ARROW
Select the menu to the left or right; or, when a submenu is visible, to switch between the main menu and the submenu	LEFT ARROW or RIGHT ARROW
Select the first or last command on the menu or submenu	HOME or END
Close the visible menu and submenu at the same time	ALT
Close the visible menu; or, with a submenu visible, to close the submenu only	ESC

Work in windows and dialog boxes

Using a program window

TASK	SHORTCUT
Switch to the next program	ALT+TAB
Switch to the previous program	ALT+SHIFT+TAB
Show the Windows **Start** menu	CTRL+ESC
Close the active database window	CTRL+W
Switch to the next database window	CTRL+F6
Switch to the previous database window	CTRL+SHIFT+F6
Restore the selected minimized window when all windows are minimized	ENTER

Using a dialog box

TASK	SHORTCUT
Switch to the next tab in a dialog box	CTRL+TAB
Switch to the previous tab in a dialog box	CTRL+SHIFT+TAB
Move to the next option or option group	TAB
Move to the previous option or option group	SHIFT+TAB
Move between options in the selected drop-	Arrow keys

down list box, or to move between some options in a group of options	
Perform the action assigned to the selected button; select or clear the check box	SPACEBAR
Move to the option by the first letter in the option name in a drop-down list box	Letter key for the first letter in the option name you want (when a drop-down list box is selected)
Select the option, or to select or clear the check box by the letter underlined in the option name	ALT+letter key
Open the selected drop-down list box	ALT+DOWN ARROW
Close the selected drop-down list box	ESC
Perform the action assigned to the default button in the dialog box	ENTER
Cancel the command and close the dialog box	ESC

Editing in a text box

TASK	SHORTCUT

Move to the beginning of the entry	HOME
Move to the end of the entry	END
Move one character to the left or right	LEFT ARROW or RIGHT ARROW
Move one word to the left or right	CTRL+LEFT ARROW or CTRL+RIGHT ARROW
Select from the insertion point to the beginning of the text entry	SHIFT+HOME
Select from the insertion point to the end of the text entry	SHIFT+END
Change the selection by one character to the left	SHIFT+LEFT ARROW
Change the selection by one character to the right	SHIFT+RIGHT ARROW
Change the selection by one word to the left	CTRL+SHIFT+LEFT ARROW
Change the selection by one word to the right	CTRL+SHIFT+RIGHT ARROW

Work with property sheets

Using a property sheet with a form or report in Design view or Layout view

TASK	SHORTCUT
Show or hide the Property Sheet	F4
Move among choices in the control selection drop-down list one item at a time	DOWN ARROW or UP ARROW
Move among choices in the control selection drop-down list one page at a time	PAGE DOWN or PAGE UP
Move to the property sheet tabs from the control selection drop-down list	TAB
Move among the property sheet tabs with a tab selected, but no property selected	LEFT ARROW or RIGHT ARROW
With a property already selected, move down one property on a tab	TAB
With a property selected, move up one property on a tab; or if already at the top, move to the tab	SHIFT+TAB
Toggle forward between tabs when a property is selected	CTRL+TAB
Toggle backward between tabs when a property is selected	CTRL+SHIFT+TAB

Using a property sheet with a table or query in Design view

TASK	SHORTCUT
Show or hide the Property Sheet	F4
With a tab selected, but no property selected, move among the property sheet tabs	LEFT ARROW or RIGHT ARROW
Move to the property sheet tabs when a property is selected	CTRL+TAB
Move to the first property of a tab when no property is selected	TAB
Move down one property on a tab	TAB
Move up one property on a tab; or if already at the top, select the tab itself	SHIFT+TAB
Toggle forward between tabs when a property is selected	CTRL+TAB
Toggle backward between tabs when a property is selected	CTRL+SHIFT+TAB

Using the Field List pane with a form or report in Design view or Layout view

TASK	SHORTCUT
Show or hide the **Field List** pane	ALT+F8
Add the selected field to the form or report detail section	ENTER

Move up or down the **Field List** pane	UP ARROW or DOWN ARROW
Move between the upper and lower panes of the **Field List**	TAB

Shortcut Keys For Working With Text And Data In Access.

Select text and data

Selecting text in a field

TASK	SHORTCUT
Change the size of the selection by one character to the right	SHIFT+RIGHT ARROW
Change the size of the selection by one word to the right	CTRL+SHIFT+RIGHT ARROW
Change the size of the selection by one character to the left	SHIFT+LEFT ARROW
Change the size of the selection by one word to the left	CTRL+SHIFT+LEFT ARROW

Selecting a field or record

Note: To cancel a selection, use the opposite arrow key.

TASK	SHORTCUT
Select the next field	TAB

Switch between Edit mode (with insertion point displayed) and Navigation mode in a datasheet. When using a form or report, press ESC to leave Navigation mode.	F2
Switch between selecting the current record and the first field of the current record, in Navigation mode	SHIFT+SPACEBAR
Extend selection to the previous record, if the current record is selected	SHIFT+UP ARROW
Extend selection to the next record, if the current record is selected	SHIFT+DOWN ARROW
Select all records	CTRL+A or CTRL+SHIFT+SPACEBAR

Extending a selection

TASK	SHORTCUT
Turn on Extend mode (in Datasheet view, **Extended Selection** appears in the lower-right corner of the window); pressing F8 repeatedly extends the	F8

selection to the word, the field, the record, and all records	
Extend a selection to adjacent fields in the same row in Datasheet view	LEFT ARROW or RIGHT ARROW
Extend a selection to adjacent rows in Datasheet view	UP ARROW or DOWN ARROW
Undo the previous extension	SHIFT+F8
Cancel Extend mode	ESC

Selecting and moving a column in Datasheet view

TASK	SHORTCUT
Select the current column or cancel the column selection, in Navigation mode only	CTRL+SPACEBAR
Extend the selection one column to the right, if the current column is selected	SHIFT+RIGHT ARROW
Extend the selection one column to the left, if the current column is selected	SHIFT+LEFT ARROW
Turn on Move mode; then press the RIGHT ARROW or LEFT ARROW key to move selected column(s) to the right or left	CTRL+SHIFT+F8

Edit text and data

Note: If the insertion point is not visible, press F2 to display it.

Moving the insertion point in a field

TASK	SHORTCUT
Move the insertion point one character to the right	RIGHT ARROW
Move the insertion point one word to the right	CTRL+RIGHT ARROW
Move the insertion point one character to the left	LEFT ARROW
Move the insertion point one word to the left	CTRL+LEFT ARROW
Move the insertion point to the end of the field, in single-line fields; or to move it to the end of the line in multi-line fields	END
Move the insertion point to the end of the field, in multiple-line fields	CTRL+END
Move the insertion point to the beginning of the field, in single-line fields; or to move it to the beginning of the line in multi-line fields	HOME
Move the insertion point to the beginning of the field, in multiple-line fields	CTRL+HOME

Copying, moving, or deleting text

TASK	SHORTCUT

Copy the selection to the Clipboard	CTRL+C
Cut the selection and copy it to the Clipboard	CTRL+X
Paste the contents of the Clipboard at the insertion point	CTRL+V
Delete the selection or the character to the left of the insertion point	BACKSPACE
Delete the selection or the character to the right of the insertion point	DELETE
Delete all characters to the right of the insertion point	CTRL+DELETE

Undoing changes

TASK	SHORTCUT
Undo typing	CTRL+Z or ALT+BACKSPACE
Undo changes in the current field or current record; if both have been changed, press ESC twice to undo changes, first in the current field and then in the current record	ESC

Entering data in Datasheet or Form view

TASK	SHORTCUT
Insert the current date	CTRL+SEMICOLON (;)
Insert the current time	CTRL+SHIFT+COLON (:)

Insert the default value for a field	CTRL+ALT+SPACEBAR
Insert the value from the same field in the previous record	CTRL+APOSTROPHE (')
Add a new record	CTRL+PLUS SIGN (+)
In a datasheet, delete the current record	CTRL+MINUS SIGN (-)
Save changes to the current record	SHIFT+ENTER
Switch between the values in a check box or option button	SPACEBAR
Insert a new line in a Short Text or Long Text field	CTRL+ENTER

Refreshing fields with current data

TASK	SHORTCUT
Recalculate the fields in the window	F9
Requery the underlying tables; in a subform, this requires the underlying table for the subform only	SHIFT+F9
Refresh the contents of a Lookup field list box or combo box	F9

Shortcut Keys For Navigating Records In Access.

Navigate in Design view

TASK	SHORTCUT

Switch between Edit mode (with insertion point displayed) and Navigation mode	F2
Toggle the property sheet	F4 or ALT+ENTER
Switch to Form view from form Design view	F5
Switch between the upper and lower portions of a window (Design view of macros, queries, and the Advanced Filter/Sort window) Use F6 when the TAB key does not take you to the section of the screen you want.	F6
Toggle forward between the design pane, properties, Navigation Pane, access keys, and Zoom controls (Design view of tables, forms, and reports)	F6
Open the Visual Basic Editor from a selected property in the property sheet for a form or report	F7
Invokes the **Field List** pane in a form, or report. If the **Field List** pane is already open, focus moves to the **Field List** pane.	ALT+F8
When you have a code module open, switch from the Visual Basic Editor to form or report Design view	SHIFT+F7
Switch from a control's property sheet in form or report Design	SHIFT+F7

view to the design surface without changing the control focus	
Copy the selected control to the Clipboard	CTRL+C
Cut the selected control and copy it to the Clipboard	CTRL+X
Paste the contents of the Clipboard in the upper-left corner of the selected section	CTRL+V
Move the selected control to the right by a pixel along the page's grid	RIGHT ARROW
Move the selected control to the left by a pixel along the page's grid	LEFT ARROW
Move the selected control up by a pixel along the page's grid **Note:** For controls in a stacked layout, this switches the position of the selected control with the control directly above it, unless it is already the uppermost control in the layout.	UP ARROW
Move the selected control down by a pixel along the page's grid **Note:** For controls in a stacked layout, this switches the position of the selected control with the control directly below it, unless it is already the lowermost control in the layout.	DOWN ARROW

Move the selected control to the right by a pixel (irrespective of the page's grid)	CTRL+RIGHT ARROW
Move the selected control to the left by a pixel (irrespective of the page's grid)	CTRL+LEFT ARROW
Move the selected control up by a pixel (irrespective of the page's grid) **Note:** For controls in a stacked layout, this switches the position of the selected control with the control directly above it, unless it is already the uppermost control in the layout.	CTRL+UP ARROW
Move the selected control down by a pixel (irrespective of the page's grid) **Note:** For controls in a stacked layout, this switches the position of the selected control with the control directly below it, unless it is already the lowermost control in the layout.	CTRL+DOWN ARROW
Increase the width of the selected control (to the right) by a pixel **Note:** For controls in a stacked layout, this increases the width of the whole layout.	SHIFT+RIGHT ARROW

Decrease the width of the selected control (to the left) by a pixel. **Note:** For controls in a stacked layout, this decreases the width of the whole layout.	SHIFT+LEFT ARROW
Decrease the height of the selected control (from the bottom) by a pixel	SHIFT+UP ARROW
Increase the height of the selected control (from the bottom) by a pixel	SHIFT+DOWN ARROW

Navigate in Datasheet view

Going to a specific record

TASK	SHORTCUT
Move to the record number box; then type the record number and press ENTER	F5

Navigating between fields and records

TASK	SHORTCUT
Move to the next field	TAB or RIGHT ARROW
Move to the last field in the current record, in Navigation mode	END
Move to the previous field	SHIFT+TAB, or LEFT ARROW

Move to the first field in the current record, in Navigation mode	HOME
Move to the current field in the next record	DOWN ARROW
Move to the current field in the last record, in Navigation mode	CTRL+DOWN ARROW
Move to the last field in the last record, in Navigation mode	CTRL+END
Move to the current field in the previous record	UP ARROW
Move to the current field in the first record, in Navigation mode	CTRL+UP ARROW
Move to the first field in the first record, in Navigation mode	CTRL+HOME

Navigating to another screen of data

TASK	SHORTCUT
Move down one screen	PAGE DOWN
Move up one screen	PAGE UP
Move right one screen	CTRL+PAGE DOWN
Move left one screen	CTRL+PAGE UP

Navigate in subdatasheets

Going to a specific record

TASK	SHORTCUT

Move from the subdatasheet to move to the record number box; then type the record number and press ENTER	ALT+F5

Expanding and collapsing subdatasheet

TASK	SHORTCUT
Move from the datasheet to expand the record's Subdatasheet	CTRL+SHIFT+DOWN ARROW
Collapse the Subdatasheet	CTRL+SHIFT+UP ARROW

Navigating between the datasheet and subdatasheet

TASK	SHORTCUT
Enter the subdatasheet from the last field of the previous record in the datasheet	TAB
Enter the subdatasheet from the first field of the following record in the datasheet	SHIFT+TAB
Exit the subdatasheet and move to the first field of the next record in the datasheet	CTRL+TAB
Exit the subdatasheet and move to the last field of the previous record in the datasheet	CTRL+SHIFT+TAB
From the last field in the subdatasheet to enter the next field in the datasheet	TAB

From the datasheet to bypass the subdatasheet and move to the next record in the datasheet	DOWN ARROW
From the datasheet to bypass the subdatasheet and move to the previous record in the datasheet	UP ARROW

Note: You can navigate between fields and records in a subdatasheet with the same shortcut keys used in Datasheet view.

Navigate in Form view

Going to a specific record

TASK	SHORTCUT
Move to the record number box; then type the record number and press ENTER	F5

Navigating between fields and records

TASK	SHORTCUT
Move to the next field	TAB
Move to the previous field	SHIFT+TAB
Move to the last control on the form and remain in the current record, in Navigation mode	END
Move to the last control on the form and set focus in the last record, in Navigation mode	CTRL+END

Move to the first control on the form and remain in the current record, in Navigation mode	HOME
Move to the first control on the form and set focus in the first record, in Navigation mode	CTRL+HOME
Move to the current field in the next record	CTRL+PAGE DOWN
Move to the current field in the previous record	CTRL+PAGE UP

Navigating in forms with more than one page

TASK	SHORTCUT
Move down one page; at the end of the record, moves to the equivalent page on the next record	PAGE DOWN
Move up one page; at the end of the record, moves to the equivalent page on the previous record	PAGE UP

Navigating between a main form and a subform

TASK	SHORTCUT
Enter the subform from the preceding field in the main form	TAB
Enter the subform from the following field in the main form	SHIFT+TAB
Exit the subform and move to the next field in the master form or next record	CTRL+TAB

Exit the subform and move to the previous field in the main form or previous record	CTRL+SHIFT+TAB

Navigate in Print Preview and Layout Preview

Dialog box and window operations

TASK	SHORTCUT
Open the **Print** dialog box from Print	CTRL+P (for datasheets, forms, and reports)
Open the **Page Setup** dialog box (forms and reports only)	S
Zoom in or out on a part of the page	Z
Cancel Print Preview or Layout Preview	C or ESC

Viewing different pages

TASK	SHORTCUT
Move to the page number box; then type the page number and press ENTER	ALT+F5
View the next page (when **Fit To Window** is selected)	PAGE DOWN or DOWN ARROW
View the previous page (when **Fit To Window** is selected)	PAGE UP or UP ARROW

Navigating in Print Preview and Layout Preview

TASK	SHORTCUT
Scroll down in small increments	DOWN ARROW
Scroll down one full screen	PAGE DOWN
Move to the bottom of the page	CTRL+DOWN ARROW
Scroll up in small increments	UP ARROW
Scroll up one full screen	PAGE UP
Move to the top of the page	CTRL+UP ARROW
Scroll to the right in small increments	RIGHT ARROW
Move to the right edge of the page	END
Move to the lower-right corner of the page	CTRL+END
Scroll to the left in small increments	LEFT ARROW
Move to the left edge of the page	HOME
Move to the upper-left corner of the page	CTRL+HOME

Any Pane

TASK	SHORTCUT
Move among the Query Designer panes	F6, SHIFT+F6

Diagram Pane

TASK	SHORTCUT

Move among tables, views, and functions, (and to join lines, if available)	TAB, or SHIFT+TAB
Move between columns in a table, view, or function	Arrow keys
Choose the selected data column for output	SPACEBAR or PLUS key
Remove the selected data column from the query output	SPACEBAR or MINUS key
Remove the selected table, view, or function, or join line from the query	DELETE

Note: If multiple items are selected, pressing SPACEBAR affects all selected items. Select multiple items by holding down the SHIFT key while clicking them. Toggle the selected state of a single item by holding down CTRL while clicking it.

Grid Pane

TASK	SHORTCUT
Move among cells	Arrow keys or TAB or SHIFT+TAB
Move to the last row in the current column	CTRL+DOWN ARROW
Move to the first row in the current column	CTRL+UP ARROW
Move to the top left cell in the visible portion of grid	CTRL+HOME
Move to the bottom right cell	CTRL+END

Move in a drop-down list	UP ARROW or DOWN ARROW
Select an entire grid column	CTRL+SPACEBAR
Toggle between edit mode and cell selection mode	F2
Copy selected text in cell to the Clipboard (in edit mode)	CTRL+C
Cut selected text in cell and place it on the Clipboard (in edit mode)	CTRL+X
Paste text from the Clipboard (in edit mode)	CTRL+V
Toggle between insert and overstrike mode while editing in a cell	INS
Toggle the check box in the Output column **Note:** If multiple items are selected, pressing this key affects all selected items.	SPACEBAR
Clear the selected contents of a cell	DELETE
Clear all values for a selected grid column	DELETE

SQL Pane

You can use the standard Windows editing keys when working in the SQL pane, such as CTRL+ arrow keys to move between words, and the **Cut**, **Copy**, and **Paste** commands on the **Home** tab.

Note: You can only insert text; there is no overstrike mode.

Shortcut Keys For Access Ribbon Commands

Ribbon keyboard shortcuts

1. Press ALT.
   The KeyTips are displayed over each feature that is available in the current view.
2. Press the letter shown in the KeyTip over the feature that you want to use.
3. Depending on which letter you press, you might be shown additional KeyTips. For example, if the **External Data** tab is active and you press C, the **Create** tab is displayed, along with the KeyTips for the groups on that tab.
4. Continue pressing letters until you press the letter of the command or control that you want to use. In some cases, you must first press the letter of the group that contains the command.

Note: To cancel the action that you are taking and hide the KeyTips, press ALT.

Online Help

Keyboard shortcuts for using the Help window

The Help window provides access to all Office Help content. The Help window displays topics and other Help content.

In the Help window

TASK	SHORTCUT
Open the Help window.	F1
Switch between the Help window and the active program.	ALT+TAB
Go back to **Program Name** Home.	ALT+HOME
Select the next item in the Help window.	TAB
Select the previous item in the Help window.	SHIFT+TAB
Perform the action for the selected item.	ENTER
In the **Browse Program Name Help** section of the Help window, select the next or previous item, respectively.	TAB or SHIFT+TAB
In the **Browse Program Name Help** section of the Help window, expand or collapse the selected item, respectively.	ENTER
Select the next hidden text or hyperlink, including **Show All** or **Hide All** at the top of a topic.	TAB
Select the previous hidden text or hyperlink.	SHIFT+TAB
Perform the action for the selected **Show All**, **Hide All**, hidden text, or hyperlink.	ENTER

Move back to the previous Help topic (**Back** button).	ALT+LEFT ARROW or BACKSPACE
Move forward to the next Help topic (**Forward** button).	ALT+RIGHT ARROW
Scroll small amounts up or down, respectively, within the currently displayed Help topic.	UP ARROW, DOWN ARROW
Scroll larger amounts up or down, respectively, within the currently displayed Help topic.	PAGE UP, PAGE DOWN
Stop the last action (**Stop** button).	ESC
Refresh the window (**Refresh** button).	F5
Print the current Help topic. **Note:** If the cursor is not in the current Help topic, press F6, and then press CTRL+P.	CTRL+P
Change the connection state.	F6, and then press ENTER to open the list of choices
Switch among areas in the Help window; for example, switch between the toolbar and the **Search** list.	F6
In a Table of Contents in tree view, select the next or previous item, respectively.	UP ARROW, DOWN ARROW

In a Table of Contents in tree view, expand or collapse the selected item, respectively.	LEFT ARROW, RIGHT ARROW

Microsoft Office basics

Use Open and Save As in the Backstage

TASK	SHORTCUT
View **Open** in the Backstage.	Ctrl+O
View **Save As** in the Backstage.	Ctrl+S
Continue saving an Office file (after giving the file a name and location)	Ctrl+S
View **Save As** in the Backstage (after giving the file a name and location)	Alt+F+S
Return to your Office file.	Esc

Use the Open and Save As dialog boxes

TASK	SHORTCUT
View the **Open** dialog box.	Ctrl+F12
View the **Save As** dialog box.	F12
Open the selected folder or file.	ENTER
Open the folder one level above the selected folder.	BACKSPACE
Delete the selected folder or file.	DELETE
Display a shortcut menu for a selected item such as a folder or file.	SHIFT+F10
Move forward through options.	TAB
Move back through options.	SHIFT+TAB
Open the **Look in** list.	F4 or ALT+I

Display and use windows

TASK	SHORTCUT
Switch to the next window.	ALT+TAB
Switch to the previous window.	ALT+SHIFT+TAB
Close the active window.	CTRL+W or CTRL+F4
Move to a task pane from another pane in the program window (clockwise direction). You might need to press F6 more than once. **Note:** If pressing F6 doesn't display the task pane you want, try pressing ALT to place focus on the ribbon and then pressing CTRL+TAB to move to the task pane.	F6
When more than one window is open, switch to the next window.	CTRL+F6
Switch to the previous window.	CTRL+SHIFT+F6
When a document window is not maximized, perform the **Size** command (on the **Control** menu for the window). Press the arrow keys to resize the window, and, when finished, press ENTER.	CTRL+F8
Minimize a window to an icon (works for only some Microsoft Office programs).	CTRL+F9
Maximize or restore a selected window.	CTRL+F10

Copy a picture of the screen to the Clipboard.	PRINT SCREEN
Copy a picture of the selected window to the Clipboard.	ALT+PRINT SCREEN

Move around in text or cells

TASK	SHORTCUT
Move one character to the left.	LEFT ARROW
Move one character to the right.	RIGHT ARROW
Move one line up.	UP ARROW
Move one line down.	DOWN ARROW
Move one word to the left.	CTRL+LEFT ARROW
Move one word to the right.	CTRL+RIGHT ARROW
Move to the end of a line.	END
Move to the beginning of a line.	HOME
Move up one paragraph.	CTRL+UP ARROW
Move down one paragraph.	CTRL+DOWN ARROW
Move to the end of a text box.	CTRL+END
Move to the beginning of a text box.	CTRL+HOME
Repeat the last **Find** action.	SHIFT+F4

Move around in and work in tables

TASK	SHORTCUT
Move to the next cell.	TAB

Move to the preceding cell.	SHIFT+TAB
Move to the next row.	DOWN ARROW
Move to the preceding row.	UP ARROW
Insert a tab in a cell.	CTRL+TAB
Start a new paragraph.	ENTER
Add a new row at the bottom of the table.	TAB at the end of the last row

Access and use task panes

TASK	SHORTCUT
Move to a task pane from another pane in the program window. (You might need to press F6 more than once.) **Note:** If pressing F6 doesn't display the task pane you want, try pressing ALT to place the focus on the ribbon and then pressing CTRL+TAB to move to the task pane.	F6
When a task pane is active, select the next or previous option in the task pane.	TAB or SHIFT+TAB
Display the full set of commands on the task pane menu.	CTRL+DOWN ARROW
Move among choices on a selected submenu; move among certain options in a group of options in a dialog box.	DOWN ARROW or UP ARROW

Open the selected menu, or perform the action assigned to the selected button.	SPACEBAR or ENTER
Open a shortcut menu; open a drop-down menu for the selected gallery item.	SHIFT+F10
When a menu or submenu is visible, select the first or last command on the menu or submenu.	HOME or END
Scroll up or down in the selected gallery list.	PAGE UP or PAGE DOWN
Move to the top or bottom of the selected gallery list.	CTRL+HOME or CTRL+END

Tips

Use dialog boxes

TASK	SHORTCUT
Move to the next option or option group.	TAB
Move to the previous option or option group.	SHIFT+TAB
Switch to the next tab in a dialog box.	CTRL+TAB
Switch to the previous tab in a dialog box.	CTRL+SHIFT+TAB
Move between options in an open drop-down list, or between options in a group of options.	Arrow keys

Perform the action assigned to the selected button; select or clear the selected check box.	SPACEBAR
Open the list if it is closed and move to that option in the list.	First letter of an option in a drop-down list
Select an option; select or clear a check box.	ALT+ the letter underlined in an option
Open a selected drop-down list.	ALT+DOWN ARROW
Close a selected drop-down list; cancel a command and close a dialog box.	ESC
Perform the action assigned to a default button in a dialog box.	ENTER

Use edit boxes within dialog boxes

An edit box is a blank in which you type or paste an entry, such as your user name or the path of a folder.

TASK	SHORTCUT
Move to the beginning of the entry.	HOME
Move to the end of the entry.	END
Move one character to the left or right.	LEFT ARROW or RIGHT ARROW
Move one word to the left.	CTRL+LEFT ARROW

Move one word to the right.	CTRL+RIGHT ARROW
Select or cancel selection one character to the left.	SHIFT+LEFT ARROW
Select or cancel selection one character to the right.	SHIFT+RIGHT ARROW
Select or cancel selection one word to the left.	CTRL+SHIFT+LEFT ARROW
Select or cancel selection one word to the right.	CTRL+SHIFT+RIGHT ARROW
Select from the insertion point to the beginning of the entry.	SHIFT+HOME
Select from the insertion point to the end of the entry.	SHIFT+END

Customer's Page.

This page is for customers who enjoyed Microsoft Access 2016 Keyboard Shortcuts For Windows.

Dearly beloved customer, please leave a review behind if you enjoyed this book or found it helpful. It will be highly appreciated, thank you.

Other Books By This Publisher.

S/N	Title	Series
Series A: Limits Breaking Quotes.		
1	Discover Your Key Christian Quotes	Limits Breaking Quotes
Series B: Shortcut Matters.		
1	Windows 7 Shortcuts	Shortcut Matters
2	Windows 7 Shortcuts & Tips	Shortcut Matters
3	Windows 8.1 Shortcuts	Shortcut Matters
4	Windows 10 Shortcut Keys	Shortcut Matters
5	Microsoft Office 2007 Keyboard Shortcuts For Windows.	Shortcut Matters
6	Microsoft Office 2010 Shortcuts For Windows.	Shortcut Matters
7	Microsoft Office 2013 Shortcuts For Windows.	Shortcut Matters
Series C: Teach Yourself.		
1	Teach Yourself Computer Fundamentals	Teach Yourself
Series D: For Painless Publishing		
1	Self-Publish it with CreateSpace.	For Painless Publishing
2	Where is my money? Now solved for Kindle and CreateSpace	For Painless Publishing
3	Describe it on Amazon	For Painless Publishing
4	How To Market That Book.	For Painless Publishing

www.ingramcontent.com/pod-product-compliance
Lightning Source LLC
Chambersburg PA
CBHW070855070326
40690CB00009B/1852